SHERLOCK HOLMES: TWO PLAYS

It is the end of the nineteenth century, and Sherlock Holmes, the world-famous detective, lives at 221B Baker Street in London. The great capital is a rainy, foggy city, where the police often have difficulty in catching criminals. Luckily, Holmes is there to help them, but only if a case is interesting enough.

Holmes is extremely intelligent, and intelligent people are often impatient with their friends. 'Think, Watson!' he says sharply to the good doctor, who is not as clever or as quick as he is. But he sometimes needs Dr Watson's help, and is grateful for it, especially in a dangerous situation.

T0021672

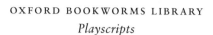

OXFORD BOOKWORMS LIBRARY

Playscripts

Sherlock Holmes: Two Plays

Stage 1 (400 headwords)

Playscripts Series Editor: Clare West

SIR ARTHUR CONAN DOYLE

Sherlock Holmes:
Two Plays

Retold by
John Escott

OXFORD UNIVERSITY PRESS

OXFORD

UNIVERSITY PRESS

Great Clarendon Street, Oxford OX2 6DP

Oxford University Press is a department of the University of Oxford.
It furthers the University's objective of excellence in research, scholarship,
and education by publishing worldwide in

Oxford New York

Auckland Cape Town Dar es Salaam Hong Kong Karachi
Kuala Lumpur Madrid Melbourne Mexico City Nairobi
New Delhi Shanghai Taipei Toronto

With offices in

Argentina Austria Brazil Chile Czech Republic France Greece
Guatemala Hungary Italy Japan Poland Portugal Singapore
South Korea Switzerland Thailand Turkey Ukraine Vietnam

OXFORD and OXFORD ENGLISH are registered trade marks of
Oxford University Press in the UK and in certain other countries

ISBN 978 0 19 423503 7

A complete recording of this Bookworms edition of
Sherlock Holmes: Two Plays is available.

Printed in China

Illustrated by: Philip Hood/Arena

For more information on the Oxford Bookworms Library,
visit www.oup.com/elt/gradedreaders

CONTENTS

The Red-Headed League   1

The Three Students   19

GLOSSARY   39

ACTIVITIES: Before Reading   42

ACTIVITIES: While Reading   44

ACTIVITIES: After Reading   46

ABOUT THE AUTHOR   50

ABOUT THE BOOKWORMS LIBRARY   51

INTRODUCTION

A strange advertisement in a newspaper is the beginning of an even stranger adventure for Sherlock Holmes and Dr Watson.

CHARACTERS IN THE PLAY

Sherlock Holmes, the famous detective
Doctor Watson, his friend and assistant
Jabez Wilson, a red-haired shopkeeper
Vincent Spaulding, Mr Wilson's assistant
Duncan Ross, a man with red hair
Mr Jones, a detective from Scotland Yard
Mr Merryweather, a bank manager
(Jabez Wilson and Duncan Ross both have red hair)

PERFORMANCE NOTES

Scene 1: Inside Wilson's shop, a room with a table and chair.
Scene 2: An office, with a table and two chairs.
Scene 3: Sherlock Holmes's room, with two chairs.
Scene 4: Outside the shop in Saxe-Coburg Square.
Scene 5: Sherlock Holmes's room.
Scene 6: The strong-room at the bank, with boxes in it.
Scene 7: Sherlock Holmes's room.

You will need a pipe, a newspaper, a walking stick, coats, hats, pens, paper, a large book, a light to carry, and two guns.

The Red-Headed League

SCENE 1

An interesting advertisement

*The inside of Wilson's shop. It's a little shop, with a lot
of clocks, pictures, watches, etc. Wilson is writing at
a table. Vincent Spaulding is looking at the* Morning
Chronicle *newspaper.*

SPAULDING This is interesting.

WILSON What is?

SPAULDING This advertisement. It is interesting for *you*,
Mr Wilson, because you have red hair.

WILSON (*Looks at Spaulding*) Go on.

SPAULDING The Red-Headed League want to find
someone new. Do you know about them? Listen.
(*Reading from newspaper*) 'To all red-headed
men, twenty-one years old or more – the Red-
Headed League can now take a new man. We pay
four pounds a week to do easy work. Come to
the League offices at 7, Pope's Court, Fleet Street,
London on Monday at 11 o'clock.' (*To Wilson*)
You can get two hundred pounds a year!

WILSON Really? Tell me about it.

SPAULDING A rich American with red hair began the

'Do you know about them?'

League. When he died, he gave a lot of his
money to the Red-Headed League, to give easy
work to men with red hair. It's very good wages
for only a little work. Why don't you go along to
Pope's Court?

WILSON But millions of red-headed men will go, and—

SPAULDING Not millions. You need to live in London.

WILSON I don't know . . .

SPAULDING And you must have *very* red hair. *You* have
very red hair, Mr Wilson.

WILSON Monday . . . eleven o'clock . . . ?

SPAULDING It's Monday today. And it's nearly eleven
o'clock! Come on!

SCENE 2
Some easy work for Wilson

The office at Pope's Court – a room with only a table and two chairs. Duncan Ross, a man with very red hair, is sitting behind the table. We can hear the noise of a lot of people out in the street.

ROSS Next!

The door opens and Spaulding and Wilson come in. Ross looks at Wilson and gets excited.

SPAULDING This is Mr Jabez Wilson, and he wants to be in the League. (*Ross gets up and walks past the table to meet them.*)

ROSS And he has a good head of hair. I can't remember when I saw a better head! (*He suddenly puts out a hand and pulls Wilson's hair.*)

Ross suddenly pulls Wilson's hair.

3

WILSON   Aaghh! Stop it!

ROSS   I'm sorry, but we must be careful. Of course it is
your hair. I can see that now. Please sit down.
Ross sits in the chair behind the table again.
Wilson sits in the other chair. Spaulding stands
behind him.

ROSS   My name is Duncan Ross. Have you got a wife,
Mr Wilson? And children?

WILSON   No, I have no wife and no family.

ROSS   Oh dear! Some of the men in our League have
lots of red-headed children. We like that.

WILSON   I'm sorry, but I—

ROSS   It's all right. You have that wonderful head of
hair. When can you begin work here?

WILSON   It's not easy. I have a shop, and—

SPAULDING   I can stay in the shop, Mr Wilson.

WILSON   What hours must I work?

ROSS   Ten o'clock to two o'clock.

WILSON   And the wages?

ROSS   Four pounds a week.

WILSON   What must I do?

ROSS   You must work here, in the office, all the time.
That is very important. You cannot go out
between the hours of ten o'clock and two o'clock.

WILSON   And the work?

ROSS   You must copy from this large book, and you must

bring paper and a pen. Can you begin tomorrow?

WILSON   Yes, I can.

ROSS   (*Smiling*) Then goodbye, Mr Jabez Wilson.
Wilson and Spaulding leave the office.

SCENE 3
Wilson tells his story

Sherlock Holmes's room. Holmes and Wilson are sitting in chairs. Holmes is smoking his pipe. Wilson has the Morning Chronicle *in his hands.*

HOLMES   Most interesting, Mr Wilson. Most interesting.
The door opens and Watson comes in.

WATSON   Holmes, I'm sorry! I didn't know—

'*Most interesting, Mr Wilson.*'

HOLMES Come in, my dear Watson! This is Mr Jabez
Wilson. He is telling me a very strange story.
(*To Wilson*) This is Doctor Watson. He's a good
friend. Give him the advertisement to read.
Wilson gives the newspaper to Watson.

HOLMES He does a lot of writing, Watson. Do you see?

WILSON Oh! How did you know that, Mr Holmes?

HOLMES The right arm of your coat is different from the
left. Your arm is on the table when you write.

WILSON (*Laughing*) Yes, that's right!

HOLMES (*Finishes reading and looks at Holmes.*) It's very
strange, Holmes.

HOLMES (*Looking excited*) It *is* strange, isn't it? Do you
see the day and month of the newspaper?

HOLMES It's the *Morning Chronicle* of 27th April, 1890.
Two months ago.

HOLMES Now, Mr Wilson, tell us about your shop.

WILSON It's in Saxe-Coburg Square, Mr Holmes. It's a
little shop, and it doesn't make much money.

HOLMES Does somebody help you in the shop?

WILSON Yes, a young man. Well, he's not *very* young, but
he works for half-wages.

HOLMES Does he! What's his name?

WILSON Vincent Spaulding. He's very good at his work.
He likes to take photographs when he's not
working. And he makes the pictures in my dark

cellar. But he works well when he's in the shop.

HOLMES How did you first see the newspaper advertisement? Tell us that.

WILSON Spaulding saw it, eight weeks ago, and we went to Pope's Court and saw Mr Duncan Ross. I told you about the visit a few minutes ago . . .

'He makes the pictures in my dark cellar.'

HOLMES Yes, yes. And I can tell Watson about it later. What happened next?

WILSON Well, I was very pleased, Mr Holmes. I went home feeling very happy. But that evening I began to think again. 'Copying from a book is strange work for a man to do,' I thought.

HOLMES Very strange, yes.

WILSON But the next morning I went to Pope's Court with my pen and some paper. Mr Ross was there, but he soon went away, and I began my work.

HOLMES Well?

WILSON I went in every morning at ten o'clock, and went home at two. And on Saturday, Ross was in the office again, and gave me my four pounds.

HOLMES How long did you work there?

WILSON Eight weeks. But today I went to the office at ten o'clock, and the door was locked. (*He takes a paper from his coat and gives it to Holmes.*) This was on the door.

HOLMES (*Reading*) 'The Red-Headed League is finished. June 23rd, 1890.' Then what did you do?

WILSON I went to the office in the next building, and I asked the man, 'What happened to the Red-Headed League?' 'Who are they?' he asked. 'Who is the man at number 7?' I asked. 'The man with the red hair?' he said. 'His name is William Morris. He moved out yesterday. He has new offices at 17 King Edward Street.' Well, I went to

King Edward Street, Mr Holmes.

HOLMES You did not find a Mr William Morris or a Mr
Duncan Ross. Am I right?

WILSON You are!

HOLMES What did you do then?

WILSON I went home to Saxe-Coburg Square.

HOLMES What does Spaulding say about all this?

WILSON He says, 'Wait for a letter. You're going to hear
something.'

HOLMES What do you think?

WILSON I need your help, I think.

HOLMES You are right, Mr Wilson. I am happy to help
you. But first I want to ask you one or two
questions. Mr Spaulding was the first to see the
advertisement. Yes?

WILSON Yes.

HOLMES When did he begin to work for you?

WILSON About three months ago.

HOLMES How did he come?

WILSON He answered an advertisement in the newspaper.

HOLMES Was he the only man to answer it?

WILSON No, twelve people answered it.

HOLMES Why did you take him?

WILSON Because he was cheap.

HOLMES He is happy to work for half the usual wages.

WILSON Yes.

HOLMES Tell me about him, this Vincent Spaulding.

WILSON He's small, and a good, quick worker. He's about thirty years old, I think.

HOLMES Where is he now?

WILSON He's at the shop.

HOLMES That is all, Mr Wilson. Today is Saturday. I am going to have an answer for you before Monday.

WILSON Thank you, Mr Holmes.

Watson goes out with Wilson. Holmes walks up and down, thinking. A minute later, Watson comes back.

HOLMES We must work quickly, Watson. Put on your hat. We're going to Saxe-Coburg Square.

SCENE 4
Holmes meets Spaulding

Outside the shop in Saxe-Coburg Square. Holmes is walking up and down. Now and then he hits the ground outside the shop with his walking stick. Then he hits the door of the shop. Spaulding opens the shop door and looks out. The legs of his trousers are dirty.

SPAULDING Can I help you?

HOLMES Yes. How can I get to the Strand?

SPAULDING Third on the right, and fourth on the left.

He goes back into the shop and closes the door.

HOLMES He's a clever young man, Watson.

WATSON He is? Why did you ask about the Strand? You know London very well! You wanted to see him.

HOLMES Not him. His trousers.

WATSON His trousers? I don't understand. And why did you hit the ground with your stick?

Holmes hits the ground outside the shop with his walking stick.

HOLMES My dear Doctor, this is not the time for talking. I must go and look at the roads behind Saxe-Coburg Square. Are you going to your work?

WATSON Yes, I must go to the hospital.

HOLMES I have things to do too. But I want your help tonight. Come at 10 o'clock. And Watson—

WATSON Yes, Holmes?

HOLMES Bring your gun.

SCENE 5
To catch a thief

Sherlock Holmes's room. Holmes, Jones and
Merryweather are talking quietly. Watson comes in.

HOLMES   Watson, you know Mr Jones of Scotland Yard.
      And this is Mr Merryweather. They're coming
      with us tonight.

JONES   Hello, Doctor. We meet again. I'm here because I
      want to catch John Clay. He's a killer and a thief,
      one of the worst men in London. It isn't going to
      be easy to catch him, because he's very clever.

HOLMES   It's after ten o'clock. We must go.

      They all leave the room.

'*He's a killer and a thief.*'

12

Scene 6
Watching and waiting

Inside the bank strong-room. There are boxes on the floor.
It is dark. The door opens and Holmes comes in, carrying
a light. Watson, Jones and Merryweather come after him.
Holmes looks carefully at the floor. Merryweather sits on a
box and hits the floor with his foot.

MERRYWEATHER How do you know— ?

HOLMES Please, no noise! Perhaps they can hear us!

JONES How long before— ?

HOLMES An hour. They are going to wait for Mr Wilson
to go to bed, then work quickly, I think. (*To
Watson*) We're in the strong-room of the First
Bank. Did you know that? Mr Merryweather
works for the bank. Tell Watson, Mr
Merryweather. What do the thieves want?

MERRYWEATHER Our gold. It's in all these boxes. Lots
and lots of it!

WATSON Gold!

HOLMES We must wait in the dark. Get behind the boxes,
everyone. Things are going to happen in the
next hour, I think. When I hear or see anything
strange, I'm going to come out quickly with a
light, and then you must help me. Be ready with

Holmes comes out from behind his box . . .

your gun, Watson. Is everything ready upstairs,
Mr Jones?

JONES My men are waiting at the front door of the
bank, Holmes. They can't get out there.

HOLMES Good. Now we must be quiet and wait.

*He puts out the light. The strong-room is dark,
but we can see the men waiting behind the boxes.
Nothing happens. Watson looks at his watch.*

WATSON (*Quietly*) It's 11.15, Holmes. When— ?

HOLMES Sshh!

*They are all quiet for nearly a minute. Then we
see a light coming through the floor. Suddenly
the ground opens. First a hand with a gun comes
out, and then Spaulding puts his other hand out.*

14

. . . and catches Spaulding.

We watch him and Ross come out.

SPAULDING (*To Ross*) Now, have you got— ?
   With his light, Holmes comes out from behind
   his box, and catches Spaulding.

SPAULDING What— !
   Ross quickly gets back into the tunnel. Jones
   wants to stop him, but he cannot. Holmes hits
   Spaulding's arm. Now the gun is on the ground.

HOLMES You can't get away, John Clay!

SPAULDING No. But my friend—

HOLMES There are three men waiting for him at the front
   door of the bank.

SPAULDING   You think of everything, Mr Holmes. You're
   very clever.

HOLMES Your Red-Headed League was clever, too. But I am pleased to catch the famous John Clay!

SCENE 7
Holmes and Watson

Sherlock Holmes's room. Holmes and Watson are sitting in chairs. Holmes is smoking his pipe.

HOLMES They needed the Red-Headed League to get Mr Wilson out of his shop. Do you understand that?

WATSON Yes, I think – er – yes.

HOLMES They wanted Wilson away from the shop for some hours every day. But how could they do it? Then Clay saw the colour of Ross's hair – and thought of a 'Red-Headed League'! When Wilson answered their newspaper advertisement, he went to work in their office every day. Then they had time to make their tunnel. Very clever!

WATSON So Spaulding is John Clay, the famous thief. When did you first know that?

HOLMES Spaulding was happy to work for half-wages. 'Why?' I thought. Spaulding often went down to the cellar. 'What's he doing down there?' I thought. Suddenly, I thought about tunnels! 'Is Spaulding making a tunnel?' I thought. 'To another building?' Watson, you saw me hitting the ground with my stick, outside the shop.

WATSON Yes . . . now I understand. Was the cellar in front of the shop? You wanted to know that.

HOLMES Yes, I did. And it wasn't. The cellar was *behind* the shop. Then I saw the man 'Spaulding'. Did you see his trousers?

WATSON Er – yes, I saw them.

HOLMES They were dirty, Watson! Why? Because making a tunnel is dirty work!

WATSON Very clever, Holmes!

HOLMES Then I went into the next street, at the back of the shop. And what did I see? The First Bank!

WATSON The bank, yes! Of course.

HOLMES 'Why is that young man making a tunnel?' I thought. 'To get into the bank strong-room!'

WATSON But why tonight? How did you know—?

HOLMES Because they closed the offices of the Red-Headed League. 'The tunnel must be ready,' I thought. And Saturday is a good day. The bank does not open on Sunday. Two days for the thieves to get away.

WATSON (*Laughing*) But they didn't get away, Holmes. You're very clever.

HOLMES (*Not laughing*) That's very true, Watson.

INTRODUCTION

Students at a college are going to take an examination very soon. But have any of them already seen the questions?

CHARACTERS IN THE PLAY

Sherlock Holmes

Doctor Watson

Hilton Soames, a teacher at St Luke's College

Bannister, a servant at the college

Gilchrist, a student

Daulat Ras, a student

Miles McLaren, a student

PERFORMANCE NOTES

Scene 1: A room with a table and chairs.

Scene 2: Soames's living room, with a writing table and chairs. There is a small table near the window. A door leads into his bedroom; a long curtain hangs near the bed.

Scene 3: Soames's living room.

Scene 4: Outside the door of Gilchrist's room.

Scene 5: Daulat Ras's room.

Scene 6: Outside the door of Miles McLaren's room.

Scene 7: The same room as Scene 1.

Scene 8: Soames's living room.

You will need a pipe, books, pens, papers, examination papers, three pieces of 'mud', pencil cuttings, and a letter.

The Three Students

Hilton Soames's story

Sherlock Holmes is sitting at a table, writing. It is evening. Watson comes in with Hilton Soames.

HOLMES (*Not looking up*) Who was at the door, Watson?

WATSON This is Mr Hilton Soames, Holmes. He teaches at St Luke's College. (*Holmes looks up.*)

SOAMES Can you give me some of your time, Mr Holmes? Today something happened at the college, and I was very worried. Then I thought, 'The famous detective, Sherlock Holmes, is visiting our town. Perhaps he can help!' And I—

HOLMES I have a lot of work to do, Mr Soames. Perhaps the police—

SOAMES No, no, I can't go to the police!

HOLMES Well, tell me your story, Mr Soames.

Watson sits down, but Soames stays standing.

SOAMES Tomorrow is the first day of an important examination, and I'm one of the examiners. Today, at three o'clock, the three exam papers arrived for me to read. Of course, every student would like to see these papers before the exam!

19

HOLMES (*Laughing*) Of course!

SOAMES We are always very careful with them. I began to read them, but at 4.30 p.m. I went out to have tea in a friend's rooms.

HOLMES Where did you leave the papers?

SOAMES They were on my writing table. I locked my door, and was away for an hour. When I arrived home, I saw a key in my door. 'Is it *my* key?' I thought. 'No, that's in my pocket. Ah, it's Bannister's key.' Bannister is my servant.

WATSON Why did he go to your room this afternoon?

SOAMES He brings my tea in every afternoon.

HOLMES But you were at your friend's rooms. Did he forget that?

SOAMES Yes. And so his key was in my door. He is usually careful, but—

HOLMES Tell me about the examination papers. Where were they when you went back to your room?

SOAMES One was on a small table next to the window, one was on the floor, and one on my writing table.

HOLMES (*Suddenly looking interested*) The first paper on the floor, the second in the window, and the third on the writing table.

SOAMES (*Opening his mouth suddenly*) Yes! How did you know that?

HOLMES (*Smiling*) Please, tell us more of your very

'When I arrived home, I saw a key in my door.'

interesting story, Mr Soames.

SOAMES First, I thought, 'Did Bannister look at the papers?' So I asked him, but he said, 'No, I did not.' And he is an honest man, Mr Holmes.

HOLMES What happened next?

SOAMES Bannister suddenly began to feel ill when I told him about the papers. He sat down on a chair and I gave him a strong drink. Then I looked carefully at the table next to the window.

WATSON What did you find?

SOAMES Small pieces of pencil.

HOLMES Did somebody break and sharpen a pencil?

SOAMES Yes, perhaps. Yes, that was it.

HOLMES Good! That helps us!

SOAMES Two more things. I have a new writing table, but

now there's a little cut on it. And there was a
piece of black mud on the table.

HOLMES Is that all?

SOAMES Yes. Please, help me, Mr Holmes!

Holmes gets up and begins to put on his coat.
Watson gets his coat and puts it on too.

HOLMES It's an interesting story, Mr Soames. Tell me,
did any student visit you in your room after the
papers arrived this afternoon?

SOAMES Yes, Daulat Ras, a student from India.

HOLMES And the papers were on your writing table?

SOAMES Yes, but he couldn't read them. He was two or
three metres away.

HOLMES But they were exam papers. Could he see that?

'There's a little cut on my new writing table.'

22

SOAMES Perhaps.

HOLMES The examination papers were in your room. Did anyone know that? Did Bannister know that?

SOAMES No, nobody.

HOLMES Where is Bannister now?

SOAMES When I ran out, to find you, Mr Holmes, he was on the chair in my room. He looked very ill.

HOLMES Did you leave your door open?

SOAMES Yes, but I locked the papers up first.

HOLMES Come, then. We must go to your rooms.

The three men leave the room.

SCENE 2
Holmes visits the college

Soames, Holmes and Watson come into Soames's living room. Holmes walks to the window and looks out.

SOAMES That window does not open, Mr Holmes. Nobody can enter the room through there.

Holmes smiles but says nothing for a minute.

HOLMES Your servant isn't here now. Perhaps he's feeling better. Which chair did you leave him on?

SOAMES The chair by the window.

HOLMES Near this little table, yes? (*He thinks for a minute.*) Yes – yes, of course. The man comes in.

23

He takes the three papers from the writing table to carry them across to the window, because . . . because then he can see you when you come across the garden to the front door, Soames!

SOAMES But he didn't see me, because I walked in through the back door.

HOLMES Ah, that helps! Can I see the three papers now? *Soames opens a box with a key and takes out the papers. Watson moves near Holmes to get a look.*

HOLMES (*Looking at the first paper*) He carries this first paper across to the table near the window and begins to copy it. It takes him – ten minutes?

WATSON Fifteen, I think.

'Can I see the three papers now?'

'Do you see the gold letters "NN"?'

HOLMES All right, fifteen. Then he puts it down on
the floor, gets the next paper, and begins to
copy that. Then he hears you coming in the
back door, Mr Soames. He must be quick! He
leaves the second paper on the table next to the
window, and runs – where? Did you hear him
running upstairs?

SOAMES No, I didn't.

HOLMES (*Looking closely at the table*) He's writing quickly,
because he breaks his pencil and needs to sharpen
it again. This is interesting. The pencil was long,
and dark blue. Look at these pieces. And do you
see the gold letters 'NN'? It's at the end of a word.
Do you know Johann Faber pencils?

WATSON I do, Holmes. I write with them.

Holmes walks across to the big writing table and

'A man can hide behind this curtain.'

takes the small piece of black mud from it.

HOLMES This is the piece of black mud? (*He looks closely at the writing table.*) I can see the cut. (*He looks across at the door.*) What is that door?

SOAMES It opens into my bedroom.

HOLMES Did you go into your bedroom before you ran out to find me?

SOAMES No.

Holmes opens the bedroom door, and looks under the bed. Then he sees the curtain.

HOLMES A man can hide behind this curtain.

He pulls the curtain back quickly. Behind it are

Soames's coats and suits. Then Holmes sees
something on the floor, under the curtain.

HOLMES What's this? It's some mud again. Your visitor
was in this room, Mr Soames.

SOAMES But – why?

HOLMES Think for a minute. He hears you coming. What
can he do? He must hide! So he runs into your
bedroom and hides behind this curtain.

SOAMES Oh! Then he was in here when Bannister and I
were in the next room!

HOLMES Yes, that's right. Tell me, how many students live
upstairs and go past your door?

SOAMES Three, all taking this examination.

HOLMES Who are they?

SOAMES There is Gilchrist. He plays football, and likes
running. His father was Sir Jabez Gilchrist. He was
a rich man, but he gambled his money away. Young
Gilchrist hasn't much money, but he works hard.

HOLMES And the Indian student?

SOAMES Yes, Daulat Ras is a quiet young man, but he
works well. Then there is Miles McLaren, a very
clever young man. But he doesn't study much
and he's worried about this examination.

HOLMES So he would like to see the papers first.

SOAMES Well . . . yes, perhaps.

HOLMES Can we speak to Bannister, your servant?

<hr>

SCENE 3

Some questions for Bannister

In Soames's living room. Holmes, Watson and Soames are sitting in chairs. Holmes is sitting at the writing table. Bannister is standing in front of him.

HOLMES Your key was in the door of this room today, Bannister. Is that right?

BANNISTER Yes, sir. I don't usually leave it there, but—

HOLMES Tell me, when did you come into the room?

BANNISTER About 4.30 p.m., sir. With Mr Soames's tea. But he wasn't here.

HOLMES Did you look at the papers on the table?

BANNISTER No, sir!

HOLMES Why did you leave the key in the door?

BANNISTER The tea things were in my hands. I thought, 'I can come back for the key.'

Mr Soames's tea.

28

WATSON Did you forget to come back?

BANNISTER Yes, sir.

HOLMES So the room was open all the time. And
somebody in the room could get in or out?

BANNISTER Yes – yes, sir.

HOLMES When Mr Soames talked to you about the
papers, you began to feel ill. So you sat down
on the chair over there. Why did you go past the
other chairs?

BANNISTER I – I don't know, sir.

HOLMES Did you stay here when Mr Soames ran out?

BANNISTER Only for a minute or two. Then I locked the
door and went to my room.

HOLMES (*To Soames*) Mr Soames, I would like to visit the
three young gentlemen. Is that all right?

SOAMES Yes, of course. These rooms are very old, and
very interesting. Visitors often go to look at them.

SCENE 4
Gilchrist

*Holmes, Soames and Watson are outside the door of
Gilchrist's room. They are looking at the doorway.*

HOLMES (*Quietly*) Remember, gentlemen, you do *not* have
a pencil with you. (*The door opens.*)

GILCHRIST What are you— ? Oh, it's you, Mr Soames.

SOAMES Gilchrist, this is Mr Holmes and his friend. They are looking at the building.

HOLMES Have you got a pencil, Watson? This is a most interesting doorway, and I want to draw it.

He takes some paper from his coat pocket.

WATSON Oh, no. I'm sorry, Holmes.

HOLMES (*To Gilchrist*) Have you, Mr Gilchrist?

GILCHRIST A pencil? Oh, yes. (*He goes away and comes back with a pencil.*) There you are, Mr Holmes. It *is* a beautiful building.

HOLMES Ah, thank you. (*He looks closely at the pencil, then draws on the paper for a minute or two.*) Yes, Mr Gilchrist, a beautiful building.

SCENE 5
Daulat Ras

Holmes, Watson and Soames are in Daulat Ras's room. The Indian is walking up and down the room. He looks worried. Holmes is drawing on a piece of paper.

HOLMES A very interesting room, Soames. (*He gives the pencil to Daulat Ras.*) Thank you, Mr Ras. (*And after a pause*) Are you . . . worried about something?

'Are you . . . worried about something?'

RAS   Sorry, what did you say? Worried? Oh, yes. It's
       the – the examination.

HOLMES Is that all?

RAS   Yes, of course. What— ?

HOLMES Good evening, Mr Ras.
       Holmes, Watson and Soames leave the room.

SCENE 6
Miles McLaren

*Holmes, Watson and Soames are outside the door of
Miles McLaren's room.*

McLAREN (*From inside the room*) Go away! I'm busy! I
        can't see anybody. Go away at once!

31

SOAMES McLaren! This is Mr—

McLAREN (*From inside the room*) Go away! It's the examination tomorrow. I must study!

HOLMES Come, my friends. It is not important.

SOAMES I'm sorry, Mr Holmes. But—

HOLMES (*Walking away*) Is he a tall young man?

SOAMES Tall? No, McLaren isn't tall. Gilchrist is the tallest of the three.

HOLMES Good. And now, Mr Soames, good night.

SOAMES What! Are you going? But tomorrow is the examination! What can I do? How—?

HOLMES I'm going to take the pieces of pencil and the mud with me. Don't worry. I'm going to come back tomorrow morning with the answer.

SCENE 7
Holmes is thinking

Holmes's room. He and Watson are sitting in chairs.

HOLMES What do you think, Watson? Who began to copy the papers?

WATSON McLaren. He said, 'Go away!' But did he want to hide something? Or perhaps . . . the student from India? Mr Ras? He looked very worried.

HOLMES Many people are worried before an examination,

Watson. It is nothing. And the pencil was no
help to us. (*He thinks for a minute.*) What about
Soames's servant?

WATSON Bannister? He's an honest man, Soames says.
That's true, I think.

HOLMES Yes. So why did an honest man . . .? Oh dear, I
must think. Where's my pipe, Watson?

SCENE 8
_____

All the answers to all the questions

*Soames's room. It is morning. A very worried Soames is
bringing Holmes and Watson into the room.*

SOAMES Well, Mr Holmes? Can we have the examination
later this morning, or must I stop it?

HOLMES You can have the examination, Mr Soames.

SOAMES But the young man—

HOLMES He isn't going to take it.

SOAMES You know him?

HOLMES Yes, I do. Please call Bannister.
Soames leaves the room.

WATSON You have the answer, Holmes?

HOLMES Yes, my dear Watson. Look. (*He opens his hand.
In it are three pieces of black mud.*)

WATSON Three! There were only two pieces of mud

33

yesterday. Where did the third piece come from?

Soames comes back into the room with Bannister.

HOLMES Now Bannister, I want the true story. What happened yesterday?

BANNISTER (*Worried*) I told you everything, sir.

HOLMES You have nothing more to say? Then I must tell you. When Mr Soames called you into the room yesterday, you saw something on that chair, and you sat on it before Mr Soames could see it.

BANNISTER No, sir!

HOLMES Yes! And when Mr Soames went out, to find me, you opened the door and said, 'You can come out now,' to the man hiding behind the curtain.

BANNISTER (*Looking afraid*) There was no man, sir.

'I told you everything, sir.'

HOLMES   That isn't true. But please go and stand next to
the bedroom door. (*He looks at Soames.*) Soames,
please go and ask young Gilchrist to come down.
Soames leaves, and comes back with Gilchrist.
Gilchrist looks worried when he sees Bannister.

HOLMES   Mr Gilchrist, there are only the five of us to hear
your answer to my question. Why did you copy
the examination papers yesterday?
Gilchrist looks at Bannister, afraid.

BANNISTER   No, Mr Gilchrist, sir! I never said anything!

HOLMES   No, but you are helping us now, Bannister. (*To
Gilchrist*) Tell us, Mr Gilchrist.
*Gilchrist suddenly begins to cry. Holmes goes
across and puts a hand on the young man's arm.*

HOLMES   You did something very wrong, Gilchrist, but
you're sorry now, I can see that. I'm going to tell
you the story, Soames. Mr Gilchrist first saw the
papers through the window.

SOAMES   But nobody can *get in* through the window!

HOLMES   That's true, but a very tall man can look through
it from the garden. (*He looks at the writing
table.*) I could not understand this cut, but then I
remembered. Gilchrist likes running!

WATSON   But . . . how does that help, Holmes?

HOLMES   Think, Watson! This young man went running
yesterday afternoon. When he walked home, his

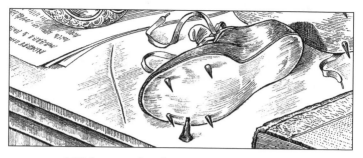

'*Gilchrist put his shoes on the writing table.*'

running shoes were in his hands . . .

WATSON And running shoes have spikes! Of course!

HOLMES Yes. Gilchrist went past this window and looked in – he's a tall young man, you see? He saw the exam papers on the writing table. Then he went past Soames's door – and saw the key in it.

WATSON And he went into the room and put his shoes on the writing table, and a spike cut into it.

HOLMES Yes, Watson. (*To Gilchrist*) What did you put on that chair near the window?

GILCHRIST My watch.

HOLMES (*To Soames*) He puts his watch on the chair, then begins to copy one of the papers. 'I'm going to see Mr Soames when he comes back across the garden,' he thinks. But you walk in through the back door, Soames.

SOAMES Then what?

HOLMES Gilchrist hears you coming, quickly takes his running shoes, and runs into your bedroom to hide. One shoe leaves some black mud behind the curtain. Is this all true, Mr Gilchrist? I found the same black mud on your shoes.

GILCHRIST Yes, sir, it's true.

SOAMES (*Angrily*) Have you nothing more to say?

GILCHRIST I – I have a letter here, Mr Soames. Early this morning, I began to write to you . . . (*He takes a letter from his pocket.*) It says, 'I'm not going to take the examination. I'm going to South Africa to work for the police there.'

SOAMES I see. You're not going to take the examination now. I'm pleased to hear that.

GILCHRIST Mr Bannister talked to me. This is the right thing to do. I understand that now.

HOLMES Gilchrist was in the bedroom, Bannister, and you didn't tell Mr Soames. When you saw Gilchrist's watch, you sat on it to hide it. Why?

BANNISTER Well, sir, I was once a servant to Sir Jabez Gilchrist, this young gentleman's father.

HOLMES Ah!

BANNISTER When he gambled his money away, I moved to the college to be a servant, but I always remembered Sir Jabez. He was good to me. So I did everything to help his son here.

HOLMES And yesterday . . . ?

BANNISTER When Mr Soames called me yesterday, I saw

Mr Gilchrist's watch on the chair. 'He looked at the examination papers!' I thought, and I quickly sat down on the watch before Mr Soames saw it.

HOLMES Then Mr Soames visited me.

BANNISTER Yes, sir, and I called young Mr Gilchrist. 'You looked at the exam papers,' I said to him. 'Did you copy them?' 'Yes,' he said. 'I did.' 'Then you cannot take the exam,' I said. 'Think of your father! He was an honest man, and you must be honest too.' I wanted to stop him, Mr Holmes.

HOLMES You were right, Bannister. Well, Soames, you have your answers now. (*To Gilchrist*) And you, young man, did wrong, but you're going to put things right. You can thank Bannister for that.

GILCHRIST I do thank him, sir.

HOLMES Come, Watson. Our work is finished here.

WATSON Yes, Holmes.

'*Our work is finished here.*'

GLOSSARY

advertisement a notice in a newspaper to tell you about something (e.g. a job)

bank a building or business where people keep their money safely

catch to find and get someone after going after them

clever quick to understand and learn

college a place where people go to study after leaving school

copy write or draw something to look like another thing

draw make pictures with a pen or pencil

examination a test of what somebody knows

examiner the person who checks the answers of an examination

floor the part of a room you walk on

gamble away lose money by betting on horses or games

gold yellow metal that is very valuable

hide get into a place where you cannot be seen

honest an honest person says only what is true, and does not take other people's things

league a number of people who agree to work or come together for a reason

lock *(v)* close something with a key; **locked** *(adj)*

paper something you write on

piece not all of something, a small part of it

police a group of men and women whose job is to see that people do not break the law

Scotland Yard a very important police station in London

servant someone who works in another person's house, cooking or cleaning

sharpen (**a pencil**)   to cut it, to make it easy to write with

sir   a polite way to speak to a man who is more important than you

story   telling about something which is true or not true

strange   surprising or not usual

strong-room   an underground room in a bank where money and gold are kept

tea   an afternoon meal

thief   a person who takes things that do not belong to him or her; **thieves** (plural)

tunnel   an underground way from one place to another

wages   the money someone pays you for doing a job

worried   afraid that something bad is going to happen

Sherlock Holmes: Two Plays

ACTIVITIES

Before Reading

1 **Read the back cover of the book, and the information on the first page. How much do you know now about Sherlock Holmes? Choose words to complete these sentences.**

1 He was born *before / after* 1900.
2 He lives in *Bath / London*.
3 He is a great *doctor / detective* and he knows it.
4 He *always / sometimes* helps the police.
5 He smokes a *pipe / cigarette* when he is thinking.
6 His *friend / brother* helps him to solve problems.
7 He is *nice to everybody / a very clever man*.

2 **Which words do you think you will find in these plays? Put a tick next to them. Why won't you find all of them?**

tunnel	college	computer
gold	dollar	careful
tea	advertisement	pencil
supermarket	airport	running shoes
bank	table	key
hair	television	mud

3 Use the clues below to complete this crossword with words from the back cover or the information on the first page. Then find the hidden six-letter word in the crossword, and say what it means.

1 When the air is thick and wet; difficult to see anything.
2 A safe place to keep money.
3 Of someone who hates waiting.
4 All the people; all the countries.
5 Strange, different from normal.
6 To find the answer to a problem.

The hidden word is _____. It means _____.

4 What is going to happen in the plays? Can you guess? Tick one box for each sentence.

	YES	NO
1 Someone loses an examination paper.	☐	☐
2 Sherlock Holmes shoots someone.	☐	☐
3 Someone tries to rob a bank.	☐	☐
4 Sherlock Holmes solves a murder.	☐	☐
5 Dr Watson marries his girlfriend.	☐	☐

While Reading

Read *The Red-Headed League*. Who says these words in the play? Who are they talking to? And who or what are they talking about?

1 'Really? Tell me about it.'
2 'I can't remember when I saw a better head!'
3 'It *is* strange, isn't it?'
4 'When did he begin to work for you?'
5 'Why did you ask about the Strand?'
6 'It's all in these boxes. Lots and lots of it!'

Match these halves of sentences, and put them together using the words below.

> *and*   *because*   *but*   *when*

1 John Clay used the name Vincent Spaulding
2 Spaulding made a tunnel to the First Bank,
3 Sherlock Holmes knew about the tunnel
4 Duncan Ross tried to get away,

5 . . . Wilson was away from the shop.
6 . . . the police were ready for him at the front door.
7 . . . got a job in Jabez Wilson's shop.
8 . . . Spaulding's trousers were dirty.

Read *The Three Students*. Choose the best question-words for these questions, and then answer them.

What / Who / Why

1 . . . did Mr Soames ask for Sherlock Holmes's help?
2 . . . brought Mr Soames's tea in every afternoon?
3 . . . did Holmes ask Gilchrist for?
4 . . . was the tallest of the three students?
5 . . . was Daulat Ras worried?
6 . . . did Gilchrist leave behind the curtain?
7 . . . did Gilchrist's letter to Soames say?
8 . . . did Bannister want to help Gilchrist?

Read Scene 8, and choose the best words to complete the passage.

A student called Gilchrist saw the papers on the *table / floor*, and came into Soames's room through the *window / door*. He put his *pen / watch* on the *chair / desk*, and *took away / copied* the paper. Suddenly he *heard / saw* Soames come in, and ran into the *bathroom / bedroom* to hide. Later, when Soames *went out / came in*, a *servant / policeman* called Bannister said to Gilchrist, 'You can come out now.' Gilchrist went *quickly / slowly* back to his room, so Soames didn't *catch / hurt* him. But Sherlock Holmes *asked about / knew* the true story. When Sherlock Holmes began to *talk / laugh* about it, Gilchrist said he was *sorry / pleased*.

After Reading

1 **Perhaps this is what three of the characters in the plays are thinking. Which characters are they, and in which play? What is happening in the play at the moment?**

   1 'Oh dear! I left the key in the door! I must be more careful next time. But wait a minute – what's that over there? Quick – I must do something to stop Mr Soames seeing it!'

   2 'It's taking a long time, and the floor's cold to sit on. Is Holmes right about this? The *police* didn't know about it! I want to be at home, having dinner with my wife! Ah, what was that noise?'

   3 'That was so easy! Of course he wants to work only four hours a day for £4 a week! What a clever idea of John's! Tomorrow we can start work in the cellar.'

2 **All these words come from *The Red-Headed League*. Put them in three groups, under these headings.**

   PEOPLE   THINGS   PLACES

   advertisement, an American, bank, book, cellar, detective, doctor, friend, hospital, letter, newspaper, office, photographs, red hair, shop, strong-room, thief, trousers

3 **Use the words below, and some of the words from your three lists, to complete this newspaper story.**

floor, free, gave, locked, pleased, say, tunnel

Yesterday the police caught a dangerous _____ and killer, John Clay. Mr Jones, a Scotland Yard _____, told us: 'He wanted to rob the First _____, so he made a _____ from the _____ of a house nearby. But we knew about his plan, so we waited for him in the _____. When he came up through the _____, we caught him and his _____. We're very _____ to have John Clay safely _____ up. He isn't going to be _____ for a very long time! I want to _____ thank you to Sherlock Holmes – he _____ us a lot of help.'

4 **Perhaps Dr Watson asked Sherlock Holmes some questions about solving the case of the three students. Match the answers to the questions and choose the right answer.**

1 Who left the key in Soames's door?
2 Why did Bannister look ill when he was in Soames's room?
3 Why did the student copy the paper near the window?
4 Where did the third piece of mud come from?

5 He was worried about Gilchrist. / He felt ill.
6 Soames did. / Bannister did.
7 Gilchrist's running shoes. / Your trousers.
8 To see Soames coming home. / To read more easily.

5 Bannister had a talk with Gilchrist before Gilchrist wrote his letter to Soames (see page 38). Write out their conversation in the correct order, and put in the speakers' names. Bannister speaks first (number 5).

1 _____ 'Yes. Did you copy the papers?'

2 _____ 'How do you know that?'

3 _____ 'Think of your father, sir! He was an honest man, and you must be honest too.'

4 _____ 'Do you? All right then, what is it?'

5 _____ 'I want to talk to you about something, sir.'

6 _____ 'Oh, I left it there, did I?'

7 _____ 'Sir, you can't take the exam now!'

8 _____ 'Yes, I must. All right. I'll write to Mr Soames.'

9 _____ 'You were in Mr Soames's room just now, sir.'

10 _____ 'Why not?'

11 _____ 'Well, I saw your watch on the chair, sir.'

12 _____ 'Yes, I did, Bannister.'

6 Here is Dr Watson, talking to a friend about Sherlock Holmes, but he says some untrue things. Can you correct them?

'Sherlock Holmes? Oh yes, he often wants me to solve crimes for him. I'm more intelligent than he is, of course. Sometimes he asks me to bring my dog with me, because there are some very dangerous animals in these cases. Come and visit us at our rooms in King Edward Street. I'm often at the office, but Holmes is usually at home.'

7 Here is a puzzle. The answer is a word from one of the plays, with seven letters. To find the word, choose the right letters (one from each sentence) and write them in the boxes.

My first is in WALK. ☐
My second is in NOISE. ☐
My third is in DIRTY. ☐
My fourth is in RIGHT. ☐
My fifth is in SPIKE. ☐
My sixth is in WAGES. ☐
My seventh is in HAND. ☐

Jabez Wilson and Hilton Soames both feel like this at the beginning of each play. What is the word?

8 Which play did you like best? Can you explain why? Write a short review of one of the plays. Use these words to help you.

I liked / didn't like this play because . . .

. . . I liked the character of _____.
. . . there was a difficult problem to solve.
. . . nobody died.
. . . I like stories about this time in history.
. . . I like detective stories.
. . . it was exciting / nothing happened.
. . . it had a good ending.

ABOUT THE AUTHOR

Sir Arthur Conan Doyle (1859-1930) was born in Edinburgh, Scotland. He studied medicine and worked as a doctor for eight years. But he needed more money, so he began writing short stories for weekly magazines.

In his first novel, *A Study in Scarlet* (1887), Sherlock Holmes appeared for the first time – a strange, but very clever detective, who smokes a pipe, plays the violin, and lives at 221B Baker Street in London. He can find the answer to almost any problem, and likes to explain how easy it is to his slow-thinking friend, Dr Watson ('Elementary, my dear Watson!'). Sherlock Holmes appeared again in *The Sign of Four* (1890), and short stories about him, in the Strand magazine, were very popular.

Conan Doyle himself was more interested in writing novels about history, like *The White Company* (1891), and he became bored with Sherlock Holmes. So, in the short story called *The Final Problem* (1893), he 'killed' him, and Holmes and his famous enemy, Moriarty, fell to their deaths in the Reichenbach falls. But Conan Doyle's readers were very unhappy about this because they wanted more stories about Holmes, so Conan Doyle had to bring Holmes back to life, in *The Hound of the Baskervilles* (1902) – perhaps the most famous of all the Sherlock Holmes stories.

There are more than fifty short stories about Sherlock Holmes. You can read them in almost any language, and there are many plays and films about the great detective.

OXFORD BOOKWORMS LIBRARY

Classics • Crime & Mystery • Factfiles • Fantasy & Horror
Human Interest • Playscripts • Thriller & Adventure
True Stories • World Stories

The OXFORD BOOKWORMS LIBRARY provides enjoyable reading in English, with a wide range of classic and modern fiction, non-fiction, and plays. It includes original and adapted texts in seven carefully graded language stages, which take learners from beginner to advanced level. An overview is given on the next pages.

All Stage 1 titles are available as audio recordings, as well as over eighty other titles from Starter to Stage 6. All Starters and many titles at Stages 1 to 4 are specially recommended for younger learners. Every Bookworm is illustrated, and Starters and Factfiles have full-colour illustrations.

The OXFORD BOOKWORMS LIBRARY also offers extensive support. Each book contains an introduction to the story, notes about the author, a glossary, and activities. Additional resources include tests and worksheets, and answers for these and for the activities in the books. There is advice on running a class library, using audio recordings, and the many ways of using Oxford Bookworms in reading programmes. Resource materials are available on the website <www.oup.com/elt/gradedreaders>.

The *Oxford Bookworms Collection* is a series for advanced learners. It consists of volumes of short stories by well-known authors, both classic and modern. Texts are not abridged or adapted in any way, but carefully selected to be accessible to the advanced student.

You can find details and a full list of titles in the *Oxford Bookworms Library Catalogue* and *Oxford English Language Teaching Catalogues*, and on the website <www.oup.com/elt/gradedreaders>.

THE OXFORD BOOKWORMS LIBRARY
GRADING AND SAMPLE EXTRACTS

STARTER • 250 HEADWORDS

present simple – present continuous – imperative –
can/cannot, *must* – *going to* (future) – simple gerunds ...

Her phone is ringing – but where is it?

Sally gets out of bed and looks in her bag. No phone.
She looks under the bed. No phone. Then she looks behind
the door. There is her phone. Sally picks up her phone and
answers it. *Sally's Phone*

STAGE 1 • 400 HEADWORDS

... past simple – coordination with *and, but, or* –
subordination with *before, after, when, because, so* ...

I knew him in Persia. He was a famous builder and I
worked with him there. For a time I was his friend, but
not for long. When he came to Paris, I came after him
– I wanted to watch him. He was a very clever, very
dangerous man. *The Phantom of the Opera*

STAGE 2 • 700 HEADWORDS

... present perfect – *will* (future) – *(don't) have to, must not, could* –
comparison of adjectives – simple *if* clauses – past continuous –
tag questions – *ask/tell* + infinitive ...

While I was writing these words in my diary, I decided what
to do. I must try to escape. I shall try to get down the wall
outside. The window is high above the ground, but I have
to try. I shall take some of the gold with me – if I escape,
perhaps it will be helpful later. *Dracula*

STAGE 3 • 1000 HEADWORDS

... should, may – present perfect continuous – *used to* – past perfect –
causative – relative clauses – indirect statements ...

Of course, it was most important that no one should see
Colin, Mary, or Dickon entering the secret garden. So Colin
gave orders to the gardeners that they must all keep away
from that part of the garden in future. *The Secret Garden*

STAGE 4 • 1400 HEADWORDS

... past perfect continuous – passive (simple forms) –
would conditional clauses – indirect questions –
relatives with *where/when* – gerunds after prepositions/phrases ...

I was glad. Now Hyde could not show his face to the world
again. If he did, every honest man in London would be
proud to report him to the police. *Dr Jekyll and Mr Hyde*

STAGE 5 • 1800 HEADWORDS

... future continuous – future perfect –
passive (modals, continuous forms) –
would have conditional clauses – modals + perfect infinitive ...

If he had spoken Estella's name, I would have hit him. I was
so angry with him, and so depressed about my future, that I
could not eat the breakfast. Instead I went straight to the old
house. *Great Expectations*

STAGE 6 • 2500 HEADWORDS

... passive (infinitives, gerunds) – advanced modal meanings –
clauses of concession, condition

When I stepped up to the piano, I was confident. It was as if I
knew that the prodigy side of me really did exist. And when
I started to play, I was so caught up in how lovely I looked
that I didn't worry how I would sound. *The Joy Luck Club*

BOOKWORMS • PLAYSCRIPTS • STAGE 1

The Butler Did It and Other Plays

BILL BOWLER

Retold by Clare West

How do you get a licence if you want to keep a monkey? What can you do if your wife has a lover? How can you see into the future? Where can you go for an exciting but cheap holiday somewhere hot and far away? How can you persuade your girlfriend or boyfriend to marry you?

The characters in these six original short plays are looking for answers to these questions. While trying to solve their problems, people get into some very funny situations. Each play gives an amusing view of life today, and there is often an unexpected ending.

BOOKWORMS • PLAYSCRIPTS • STAGE 1

Five Short Plays

MARTYN FORD

What do you do if you have a boring job in a restaurant, serving fast food to people who have no time to eat? Smile, and do your best? Perhaps it's better to find a place where time doesn't matter so much.

What if you dream of travelling to other countries, but your friends just laugh? Do you stay at home with them? Or do you decide to be more adventurous?

Perhaps you hear that someone has bought the last bag of salt in town. Do you buy a bag from him at a high price? Or try to make him give you a bag?

Our world is full of these kinds of problems. They make life interesting, and sometimes very funny. These five short plays show people trying to decide what to do in unexpected or difficult situations.

The Omega Files – Short Stories

JENNIFER BASSETT

In EDI (the European Department of Intelligence in Brussels) there are some very secret files – the Omega Files. There are strange, surprising, and sometimes horrible stories in these files, but not many people know about them. You never read about them in the newspapers.

Hawker and Jude know all about the Omega Files, because they work for EDI. They think fast, they move fast, and they learn some very strange things. They go all over the world, asking difficult questions in dangerous places, but they don't always find the answers . . .

Sherlock Holmes and the Sport of Kings

SIR ARTHUR CONAN DOYLE

Retold by Jennifer Bassett

Horseracing is the sport of kings, perhaps because racehorses are very expensive animals. But when they win races, they can make a lot of money too – money for the owners, for the trainers, and for the people who put bets on them to win.

Silver Blaze is a young horse, but already the winner of many races. One night he disappears from his stables, and someone kills his trainer. The police want the killer, and the owner wants his horse, but they can't find them. So what do they do?

They write to 221B Baker Street, London, of course – to ask for the help of the great detective, Sherlock Holmes.

BOOKWORMS • FANTASY & HORROR • STAGE 2

The Pit and the Pendulum and Other Stories

EDGAR ALLAN POE

Retold by John Escott

Everybody has bad dreams, when horrible things move towards you in the dark, things you can hear but not see. Then you wake up, in your own warm bed, and turn over to go back to sleep.

But suppose you wake up on a hard prison floor, in a darkness blacker than the blackest night. You hear the sound of water, you touch a cold metal wall, and smell a wet dead smell. Death is all around you, waiting ...

In these stories by Edgar Allan Poe, death whispers at you from every dark corner, and fear can drive you mad ...

BOOKWORMS • TRUE STORIES • STAGE 2

The Death of Karen Silkwood

JOYCE HANNAM

This is the story of Karen Silkwood. It begins with her death.

Why does her story begin where it should end? Certain people wanted her death to be an ending. Why? What were they afraid of? Karen Silkwood had something to tell us, and she believed that it was important. Why didn't she live to tell us? Will we ever know what really happened? The questions go on and on, but there are no answers.

This is a true story. It happened in Oklahoma, USA, where Karen Silkwood lived and worked ... and died.

.